I'm Thinking of a Big State

Bela Davis

Abdo Kids Junior
is an Imprint of Abdo Kids
abdobooks.com

Abdo
I'M THINKING OF A STATE
Kids

abdobooks.com

Published by Abdo Kids, a division of ABDO, P.O. Box 398166, Minneapolis, Minnesota 55439.

Printed in the United States of America, North Mankato, Minnesota.

102025

012026

THIS BOOK CONTAINS RECYCLED MATERIALS

Photo Credits: Getty Images, Shutterstock

Production Contributors: Teddy Borth, Jennie Forsberg, Grace Hansen

Design Contributors: Candice Keimig, Pakou Moua

Library of Congress Control Number: 2025936508

Publisher's Cataloging-in-Publication Data

Names: Davis, Bela, author.

Title: I'm thinking of a big state / by Bela Davis

Description: Minneapolis, Minnesota : Abdo Kids, 2026 | Series: I'm thinking of a state | Includes online resources and index.

Identifiers: ISBN 9798384907350 (lib. bdg.) | ISBN 9798384908050 (ebook) | ISBN 9798384908401 (Read-to-Me ebook)

Subjects: LCSH: States, Size of--Juvenile literature. | American states (United States)--Juvenile literature. | Geography--Juvenile literature. | Physical geography--United States--Juvenile literature.

Classification: DDC 917--dc23

Table of Contents

Guess the State! 4

I'm Thinking Of 22

Glossary 23

Index 24

Abdo Kids Code 24

Guess the State!

I'm thinking of a big state. A big state has a lot of land. It is over 100,000 square miles (300,000 sq km)!

Canada
Alaska
Canada
Montana
Nevada
Colorado
California
Arizona
New Mexico
Texas
Mexico

Can you guess the state?

The state flower is the bitterroot.

State Clues

- **Flower:** Bitterroot

7

The state bird is the western meadowlark.

State Clues

- **Flower:** Bitterroot
- **Bird:** Western meadowlark

Grizzly bears live in this state.

State Clues

- **Flower:** Bitterroot
- **Bird:** Western meadowlark
- **Animal:** Grizzly bear

This state is a good place to go skiing!

State Clues

- **Flower:** Bitterroot
- **Bird:** Western meadowlark
- **Animal:** Grizzly bear
- **Activity:** Skiing

People can visit an old west **ghost town** in this state!

State Clues

- **Flower:** Bitterroot
- **Bird:** Western meadowlark
- **Animal:** Grizzly bear
- **Activity:** Skiing
- **Visit:** Ghost town

People explore Glacier National Park in this state.

State Clues

- **Flower:** Bitterroot
- **Bird:** Western meadowlark
- **Animal:** Grizzly bear
- **Activity:** Skiing
- **Visit:** Ghost town
- **Explore:** Glacier National Park

The state's capital is Helena.

State Clues

- **Flower:** Bitterroot
- **Bird:** Western meadowlark
- **Animal:** Grizzly bear
- **Activity:** Skiing
- **Visit:** Ghost town
- **Explore:** Glacier National Park
- **Capital:** Helena

Now you have all the clues! Can you guess what state I'm thinking of?

State Clues

- **Flower:** Bitterroot
- **Bird:** Western meadowlark
- **Animal:** Grizzly bear
- **Activity:** Skiing
- **Visit:** Ghost town
- **Explore:** Glacier National Park
- **Capital:** Helena

CA
CO
AK
MT

I'm Thinking of...
Montana!

Glossary

ghost town
a town that has been deserted, especially one in the American West where gold or silver mines have closed.

national park
a special area of land that is set aside by the United States government to protect it.

Index

activities 12, 14, 16

animals 8, 10

bitterroot 6

cities 18

Glacier National Park 16

grizzly bears 10

plants 6

western meadowlark 8